To the
Rescue!™

Police Cars
Patrullas

Joanne Randolph

Traducción al español:
Eduardo Alamán

PowerKiDS press. & Editorial Buenas Letras™
New York

For Riley, Deming, and Hannah

Published in 2008 by The Rosen Publishing Group, Inc.
29 East 21st Street, New York, NY 10010

First Edition

Book Design: Greg Tucker
Photo Researcher: Nicole Pristash

Photo Credits: Cover, pp. 7, 9, 11, 13, 15, 19, 23, 24 (top right), 24 (bottom) Shutterstock.com; p. 5 © www.iStockphoto.com/David Lewis; p. 17 © Mario Villafuerte/Getty Images; p. 21, 24 (top left) by Jerome Pristash.

Cataloging Data

Randolph, Joanne.
  Police Cars–Patrullas / Joanne Randolph; traducción al español: Eduardo Alamán.— 1st ed.
      p. cm. — (To the rescue!–¡Al rescate!).
  Includes index.
  ISBN 978-1-4042-7674-1 (library binding)
  1. Police vehicles—Juvenile literature. 2. Spanish language materials I. Title.

Manufactured in the United States of America

Websites: Due to the changing nature of Internet links, PowerKids Press and Editorial Buenas Letras have developed an online list of Web sites related to the subject of this book. This site is updated regularly. Please use this link to access the list: www.powerkidslinks.com/ttr/pcar/

Contents/Contenido

Pull over! Here comes a police car!

¡Deténgase! ¡Aquí viene una patrulla!

Police cars are there to help people in need.

Las patrullas se usan para ayudar a las personas.

Police officers drive police cars. Police officers work hard to keep us safe.

Los **oficiales de policía** manejan las patrullas. Los oficiales de policía están aquí para protegernos.

A police car helps out if
there is trouble on the road.

Las patrullas ayudan a las
personas que tienen
problemas en el camino.

11

A police car is used to catch people who do bad things. The police officer takes the bad person to **jail**.

Las patrullas se usan para atrapar a las personas que han hecho algo malo. Los policías llevan a esas personas a la **cárcel**.

13

Sometimes a different kind of police car is used to bring people to jail. This car is called the paddy wagon.

A veces, se usa otro tipo de auto para llevar a las personas a la cárcel. Este camión se llama *paddy wagon*.

The police sometimes use dogs to help them save people or stop crime.

A veces, la policía usa perros para ayudarse a combatir el crimen.

A police car has lights on top. The lights are turned on when the officer needs to get someplace quickly.

Las patrullas tienen luces en el techo. Los oficiales encienden las luces cuando tienen que llegar rápido a algún lugar.

A police car has a radio, a **computer**, and more. These things help police officers do their job.

Las patrullas tienen una radio, una **computadora** y otras cosas que ayudan a los oficiales a hacer su trabajo.

The next time you see a police car, say thank you. Police cars help keep us safe.

La próxima vez que veas una patrulla dale las gracias. Las patrullas nos ayudan a estar seguros.

Words to Know/Palabras que debes saber

computer / (la) computadora

jail / (la) cárcel

police officer / (los) oficiales de policía

24